ALSO BY HANNAH HINCHMAN

A Life in Hand: Creating the Illuminated Journal

A Trail Through Leaves: The Journal as a Path to Place

Little Things in a Big Country

An Artist and Her Dog
on the Rocky Mountain Front

Little
Things
in a
Big
Country

An Artist and Her Dog
on the Rocky Mountain Front

Hannah Hinchman

W. W. Norton & Company   New York London

For information about permission to reproduce selections
from this book, write to Permissions, W.W. Norton & Company, Inc.,
500 Fifth Avenue, New York, NY 10110

Manufacturing by South China Printing Co. Ltd.
Book design, lettering and illustration by Hannah Hinchman
Production manager: Andrew Marasia

Library of Congress Cataloging-in-Publication Data

Hinchman, Hannah.
  Little Things in a Big Country: an artist and her dog on the
  Rocky Mountain Front/by Hannah Hinchman
      p. cm.
ISBN 0-393-02016-9
    1. Hinchman, Hannah. 2. Augusta Region (Mont.) – Description and
    travel. 3. Natural history – Montana – Augusta Region. 4. Outdoor
    life – Montana – Augusta Region. 5. Walking – Montana – Augusta
    Region. 6. Dogs – Montana – Augusta Region. 7. Women
    illustrators – Montana – Augusta Region – Biography. 8. Augusta
    Region (Mont.) – Biography. 9. Montana – Description and Travel. I. Title

    F739. A94 H565 2003
    917.86'615 – dc21
                                                    2003041267

W. W. Norton & Company, Inc., 500 Fifth Avenue, New York, NY 10110
www.wwnorton.com

W. W. Norton & Company Ltd., Castle House, 75/76 Wells Street,
London W1T 3QT

1 2 3 4 5 6 7 8 9 0

FOR MY MOTHER

wise and kind lover of words

Contents

ACKNOWLEDGMENTS

Alane Mason, my visionary editor at W. W. Norton, could have taken one look at this project and nixed it as too complicated, too labor-intensive, too unconventional. But she didn't; she stayed faithful to the idea and was deeply involved with every aspect of it. And thanks to agent Elizabeth Kaplan, who knew that Alane and I would work well together.

I'm grateful to Norton's production manager Andy Marasia, who so patiently worked with the heaps of illustrations and blizzards of text snippets.

My mother, my brother and my sister-in-law, masterful writers each, provided bracing comments, careful proofing and steady encouragement.

I celebrated the completion of each new chapter by taking it down to the Buckhorn Bar & Grill, where I could always find a crew ready to praise, but also point out errors of fact. Thanks especially to Lou, Gus, Kent, Frank, Beth, Ginger, Bucky, James and Tom. Special thanks to Gus Wolfe, photographer, for furnishing incomparable reference material when my own observations fell short.

It's a privilege to be able to walk freely here, and I appreciate the permission granted me by these landowners: Pat Troy, Lou Luloff, the Broken O Ranch, the Artz family, Roger King, Cottonwood Ranch, Double Creek Ranch and the Young Ranch.

After a conversation about sandhill cranes, poet John Caddy offered me the poem in Chapter Four. I'm grateful for his wonderful work and his generosity in sharing it.

Larry Lasker and Anita Keys, friends of the Dearborn, offered much design and production advice — thank you.

Eternal gratitude to Bob Kiesling, who brought me to the Front in the first place.

INTRODUCTION
Life on the Front

 moved to the Front for the country: a grand swath of prairie grassland that flows down from Canada, bounded on the west by a wall of mountains. I never expected to find a community of like-minded souls here, but to concentrate on the landscape, and let company take care of itself. So how does an aging, single, unrepentant hippie-environmentalist fit in here? She heads down to the Buckhorn Bar to flirt with all the old cowboys. That's about the only way to find out who owns what, the only way to get permission to walk, short of joining the ladies' auxiliary. And it's by far the best place to find someone to fix a fence, start a tractor or dance.

Our few pages of the regional phone book include residents within a 90-square-mile area, about 400 entries. At least there is a town center; Augusta doesn't have the sad, abandoned feeling that some Montana towns do. Not yet, anyway.

Approaching Augusta, you meet no strip of commercial development, no billboards — just lush woods and trim fields along the channels of Elk Creek, then suddenly you're on Main Street. The houses are modest boxy things, a few trailers, a few old

homestead cabins, some fine two-story Victorian gingerbreads. From mid to late summer, banks of naturalized hollyhocks bloom all over town.

I live a couple of miles north, where the creek bottom gives way to prairie, with 5 cats, a couple of horses and my dog Sisu.

Main Street lines up with a distinctive

Salty directing her nap from the director's chair.

looming volcanic intrusion called Haystack Butte. Haystack is 5 miles closer to town, not part of the Front, so it's often dramatically sunlit while storms hang over the ranges. When Haystack's summit is obscured, we know the weather has "spilled over" the mountains.

Main Street is reduced to essentials: a general store that sells everything from groceries to hip-waders, a gas station, a motel, a couple of cafés, a B & B, a hair salon, a tiny library and three bars. Then there's the anomalous Latigo & Lace, filled with original fine art from some of Montana's best artists, old prints and maps, clever gifts, a superb book selection, antiques, jewelry, local crafts, handmade clothing and a popular espresso bar. The town would feel bleak and alien without that place and the half-dozen smart women who run it.

The citizenry includes: a plutocracy of long-established ranching families and the hands who work for them. Old residents who refuse to leave for gentler climates. A pool of men-of-all-work who work when they feel like it, as carpenters, fencers, hunting and fishing guides, woodcutters. Schoolteachers for our diminishing school system. A few skilled electricians, plumbers, contractors, equipment operators. A veterinarian whose office is in the back of his pickup. A few troubled vets, a handful of hermits. Surprisingly many skilled crafts-people. As a pie chart, the town might break down like this —>

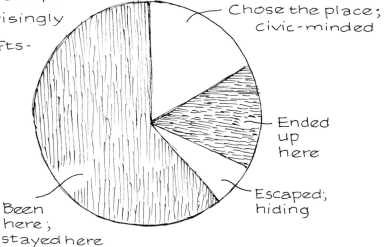

Chose the place; Civic-minded

Ended up here

Escaped; hiding

Been here; stayed here

Hats at
Latigo &
Lace

It's awfully damn lonely here, especially in winter, and the bars are the one place where you know you can find live people to talk to. My favorite, the Buckhorn, is a cozy, rustic and friendly place, dark rafters bristling with antlers. Happy hour banter at the Buckhorn, mostly sarcastic commentary on the day's paper, also runs to old stories, tales of the "characters" who used to live here. We have a number of current characters, but none of the heroic stature of the old guys who drove teams, trapped for a living, or founded ranching empires.

BUCKHORN
BAR
&
GRILL
Augusta, Montana

← COVER OF THE MENU

At first the locals branded me as a spy for the "greenies" and were wary. On further acquaintance, I've been accepted as a (mostly) harmless oddity. They recognize Sisu and me far off on the prairies, and my "rig" parked in out-of-the-way places. One friend even tests the temperature of my hood to see how long I've been out there. They know that I do art, write, and especially that I do graphic design, like the admired menu for the Buckhorn. I'm comfortable with rough men; I don't mind being teased and can dish it out in return. So I more or less "fit in".

But when it comes to issues of land, wildlife and wilderness I end up at loggerheads with the locals on all points. They believe that the world was created for humans to use, period. I believe that we are one species among many, each with a right to exist.

photographer Gus

I value the Front for its
ecological integrity;
they value it as a
source of livelihood.
(as I do in a less
direct way). They
want it domes-
ticated and
wouldn't mind
if every last
coyote,
ground
squirrel,
porcupine,
beaver, skunk,
wolf and bear
disappeared
tomorrow. I
want it wild;
that these creatures persist in healthy numbers is what
makes this place so rare and extraordinary.

On these topics I find them narrow-minded, ill-informed:
they would shred the Bayeux Tapestry for paint rags.
To them, my values are perverse, elitist, heretical.

There's no bridge across this gulf that I can find.
But we manage to talk across it, flirt across it, even
dance across it. They give me permission to roam their

land, heretic or not, bless their stubborn hearts.

I stop in at the Buckhorn to hear how calving is going, how much rain came with the last storm, the latest lion or bear sighting. I order another ton of hay from Frank, the owner (who's also a rancher), and pretty soon the drinks are stacked up in front of me and the local wits are tuning up... who wants to head back out into the windy night where it's spitting snow?

But I have a good snug home to return to, and my animals are waiting, and there are letters to write, things to put down in the journal, compelling reading matter: plenty of inducements to go home, or stay home. So I've managed to avoid the worst seductions of the bar scene, while still being counted as a "regular".

Sisu and I suit each other well. We both revere the wild, even though she's a bit more goal-oriented in her approach, an un-abashed predator. She's a Finnish Spitz, a bright, sensitive, self-contained animal. Her breed shares many char-acteristics with other Nordics, like elkhounds and malamutes, judged as "primitive" breeds in Europe, for their less-diluted wolf ancestry.

"Finkies" appear fox-like, delicate (a deception) and are only beagle-sized. The Finnish Spitz is traditionally an all-round hunting dog, ranging ahead to find and hold small game, then barking to alert its human companion.

Sisu never sits at my feet gazing up adoringly, doesn't want to sleep on the bed, squirms away from hugs, wants to be outside. She likes to be brushed and groomed—not that she needs it. She's impeccably neat. An hour after wallowing in swamp muck, she's dry, mud-free and scentless. She encourages me to extract hard-to-reach burrs, and accepts my removal of ticks. She glows, she gleams and is generally resplendent, if aloof.

Towards bedtime, though, she will roll over to have her belly rubbed, or will doze off as I lie on the floor petting her plushy ears and forehead. At least once a day she wants to wrestle with her coyote hand-puppet,

A "PLAY-BOW"

offering a "play-bow" and one of her talking yawns ("Eeee-aauuww-yow-yow") to engage me —— usually when I've just settled in with a book. And she's full of heart-rending looks when she wants a rawhide bone (rubbed with Tillamook extra-sharp cheddar).

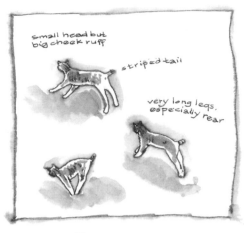

small head but big cheek ruff

striped tail

very long legs, especially rear

THE BOBCAT

When we walk in the fields around my house, dogs from the area sometimes converge on us. Their sniffing, posturing and growling are pure irritation to her. She wants quiet to hear rustlings in the brome, and to follow uncorrupted scent trails. She explores with a thorough-ness and concentration I've never seen in any other kind of dog.

I most admire her in the field, when we encounter potentially dangerous animals, like a rancher's bull, coyotes, raccoons, skunks, porcupines and once a bobcat.

She seems to know not to antagonize these.
She sits down, she watches, she waits. And yes,
she looks to me for advice about how to deal with
them. If I tell her to come away, she does. This
is a virtue where we live. A dog that chases game
animals or livestock (Sisu does neither) will sooner
or later get shot. A dog that pursues coyotes
will get eaten.

Lately I sense that she's come to appreciate my company on our excursions. It makes me feel part of a team when she stops on a ridge to look back for me. These days I can yell, "Sisu, let's go this way," and point, and she will instantly change her course to agree with mine.

Her buoyancy and eagerness are a bulwark against melancholy. She is a flying wedge of attention in whose wake I follow. I don't know what I add to her experience — she amplifies mine beyond reckoning.

CHAPTER ONE

Double Creek / Chimney Bend

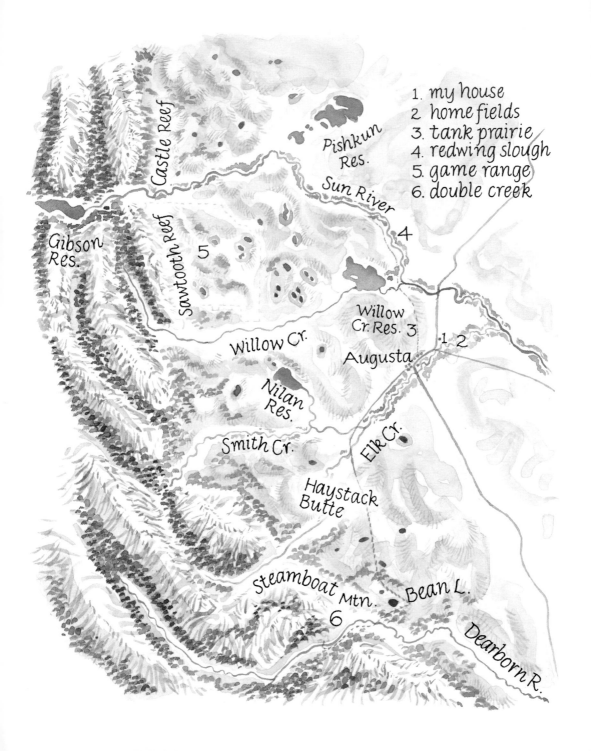

1. my house
2. home fields
3. tank prairie
4. redwing slough
5. game range
6. double creek

Castle Reef

Pishkun Res.

Sun River

Gibson Res.

Sawtooth Reef

5

Willow Cr. Res. 3

Willow Cr.

Augusta

1 2

Nilan Res.

Smith Cr.

Elk Cr.

Haystack Butte

Steamboat Mtn.

Bean L.

6

Dearborn R.

The Front is stunningly empty of people, far emptier than it was a century ago during the final homestead era. Since settlement, it has always been stock country, native mixed-grass prairie. Experiments with crops have mostly failed, except for hay and, farther to the east, barley. Across the Divide, a milder climate and the more conventional scenery of snowy peaks, pretty lakes and pointy evergreens has concentrated newcomers in the valleys around Flathead Lake and Kalispell. By contrast, the Front can seem brutal in its billowing treelessness, stark reefs and nearly constant wind.

The look of the country hasn't changed much since Meriwether Lewis passed through in 1806, rejoicing

Double Creek ~ western half

me   sisu   squirrels   solitaires   dippers   nutcrackers

at the "immence hirds of buffaloe". It's easy to imagine that a party of Blackfeet might appear on the next ridge at any moment. The bison are gone, of course, and the "vast assemblage of wolves" that Lewis saw, but wild creatures of most sorts are probably more abundant now than they have been at any time since his passage.

We are on the way to Double Creek Ranch, driving south along the mountain front on snowy gravel roads. The wall of mountains on the western horizon is an abrupt vertical axis, but it's dwarfed by the immensity of sky and prairie. Soon we'll turn west and enter the mountains via the canyon of the Dearborn River.

These great blocks of limestone (we call them "reefs") were snapped, lifted and shoved eastward to make the Front. The rows of reefs alternate with regular valleys carved out of softer rocks like shales and sandstones. At intervals the reefs are crosscut by river exits like the Dearborn.

As mountains go, these are not as high nor as steep as other ranges, but they occupy a huge area, part of a massif that extends unbroken to the Yukon, which is why this country has never been without wolves and grizzly bears. The Front is not a biological island, as the Greater Yellowstone Eco-system is.

I moved to Augusta thinking that soon I'd build a retreat-cabin on a little corner of this ranch, which runs for almost 2 miles along the south-facing bank of the Dearborn. So far I've only restored the cabin-site meadow, once engulfed by seedling firs.

Double Creek is "behind the wall", inside the mountains. Its eastern end is a last echo of the prairie grassland. Toward the western boundary, canyon walls and forest close in, and there the river does some impressive carving. We park at the beautiful new barns and walk west.

SISU DIMINUTIVE BESIDE MAT JUNIPER — A FIR SEEDLING HAS SPROUTED IN ITS SHELTER

Clingers and creepers succeed here. Species that spread out along the ground, like the mat-forming junipers and the ubiquitous Kinnikinnick create their own sheltered microclimates.

CREEPING JUNIPER

GROUND JUNIPER

Colors of
creeping juniper
in winter:
olive bronze
gray russet
chalky blue
dijon gold

A juniper laden
with berries
will appear
wholly blue
at a distance.

They add little
growth at the
edges each year,
yet some junipers
at Double Creek
are 30 feet in
diameter.

Small animal
trails, worn to
smoothness,
radiate
from them.

PLACE
WHERE A
MOUNTAIN LION
MIGHT RECLINE

ROOTS MUST
ONCE HAVE
BEEN
COVERED,
PROTECTED
BY ROCK
JOINTS.
NOW ONLY THE
LIVING TIPS
FIND CREVICES;
THE REST OF
THE ROOT IS
EXPOSED AND
TOUGHENED.

I'm poor company
when walking, so
I rarely invite
people. Indoor con-
versations seem in-
appropriate outdoors.
Any sustained talk does
— like chatting through a play. Even
if the topic is what's right in front of us. Questions, spec-
ulations, names, obligatory admiration...the scrim of
language makes me feel tired and blurred. The ideal human
companion would behave like a dog: be fully engaged in
present exploration, pursue his own course, indicate
things of interest without discussing them to death, let
out the occasional yelp of discovery. Sisu's only failing
as a companion is that we can't, in the evening over a
mug of tea, talk about our memorable day.

In Finland, Sisu's breed specializes in hunting forest game birds, especially the capercaille. But she's a dog of the American West and has developed her own tastes. Grouse don't interest her so far, but the distant crow of a pheasant does. She's rather tender toward ducks on a pond. Eagles in flight alarm her, geese merit a nod, songbirds don't register. It's the dipper, or water ouzel, rocketing along a river corridor like this, that excites heroic endeavor. She designs elaborate stalks that involve multiple river crossings and strategic use of cover.

AROUND THE BEND

See how much the river's fallen since the initial freeze-up.

Abandoned ice shelves full of glacier hues break and bend how under their own weight. In the riffles, ice nodules and lobes form on the shelf edges, the result of random splashings. Ice parapets, hoodoos and bridges — Sisu crosses the latter at a gallop, one paw-print ahead of the collapse. Sloping ice shelves are her Waterloo: inexorable entry, no exit.

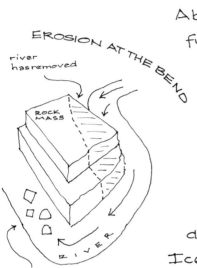

EROSION AT THE BEND

river has removed

ROCK MASS

RIVER

boulders deposited

Cleavage planes obey crystal lattices
Arrested shallows, a mild archaic beach

Hairline fractures ping into cracks
Ice and lichen broker mineral solvency

Great plates held by the merest of molecular affinities
Bewildering warehouses of eons, vast libraries of events

Ever smaller fragments, true to their structure to the end
All rendered through the dazzling equation of the present

IF A SQUIRREL IS SCOLDING FROM A TREE IT'S TOO LATE FOR PURSUIT. SHE'S LISTENING FOR THE RUSTLE OF A SQUIRREL ON THE GROUND.

Sisu's alertness is a continuous joy to me — she's never dull or "elsewhere". I cue to her expanded spectrum of senses. In turn, she's learned to pay attention when I say, "Sisu, look!", and will gaze in the direction I'm pointing. But it better be worth the diversion.

I've passed by and over the exposed rock layers at Chimney Bend before. Today I gain a new sense of their massive and highly ordered 3-dimensionality. I can feel the opposing forces at work in them and recognize the planes that govern their disintegration. The ripply pink sandstone gets exposed in broad sheets because it's so hard.

The shaley layers (some paper-thin) are
shattered before they ever reach the
surface. You can see how recently an
area was uncovered: fresh rock faces
are vividly colored and lichen-free.
Every older surface, every
fissure, becomes a nursery
for some minute plant.

AFTER THE WALK

chomp, grind, gnaw

Back home. Sisu has
done enough drift-
busting today to
wear her out. But
her sleep is so
restorative that
she'll be ready to go
again by evening —
which isn't far off.
Oh, the dearth of light here
in winter, it makes me a little
desperate, especially if I don't
have a good book waiting. There's
always darts at the Buckhorn, but
that requires some
gussying-up, and
tonight I'm unwill-
ing. This will be a
letter-and-journal
night. Communica-
tive, if remotely.

sigh....

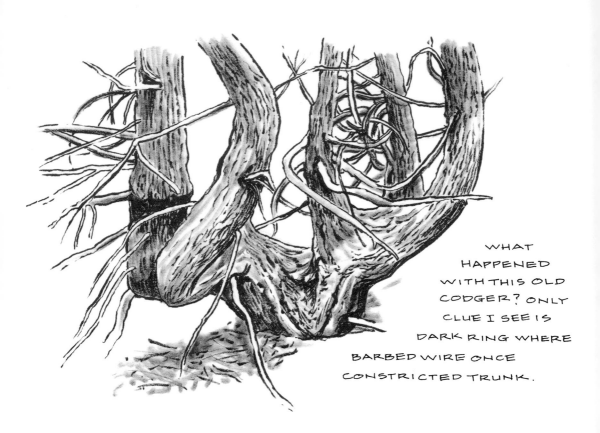

WHAT HAPPENED WITH THIS OLD CODGER? ONLY CLUE I SEE IS DARK RING WHERE BARBED WIRE ONCE CONSTRICTED TRUNK.

Season of party-horn notes of red-breasted nuthatches. Season of sun finally cresting Twin Buttes to penetrate river corridor. Season of junipers in their true color glory. Season of laid-back dart-playing ranchers before calving begins. Day of being dressed ideally, especially instantly comfortable new hiking boots. Day of angularity (cleavage-planed rock blocks) vs. curvaceousness (ice formations). Day of finding singular trees.

CHAPTER TWO

Home Fields

sheep pasture with big trees

huge new beaver dam

bank beaver lodge

good stream crossing

cows

multi-colored sheep

woods with little underbrush

slough

eagles

eagle bend

Elk Creek

houses of family that owns hay trails

(Can be seen from here)

deer skeleton

eagles

avenue

picnic ground

wet meadow

avenue

field growing up in saplings

dense woods

rabbit tree

slough

pond

great horned owl's nest

garden

willow thicket

hay corral

voles

the big hay meadow

the long field

Shorty & Darlene

Gordon & Frances

irrigation ditch

brush

unmowed fields

x squirrels

my house

many deer cross here

To Augusta →

x I ground squirrels

corral & barn

my (over)grazed field

Shorty's pasture

← To Choteau

big ground squirrel colony

E — S / N — W / mountains

Prairie Pasture

Watch 3 bald eagles in flight. One dives on another, which drops whatever it was carrying, and the third swoops in to retrieve it. A certain exuberance makes this look like play.

To Great Falls

The rancher who owns these fields and woods is a gentle man, and he takes impeccable care of them. Soon his elderly father will be out piling up the cottonwood branches that blewdown over the winter.

A still, murky day at the end of winter, when the creek ice turns opaque and creek water rises to flow over it. Cows are doubtful about crossing.

Season of willows coloring up. Season of magpies carrying sticks for nest. Emergence of the first ground squirrels, foul-tempered males. This is the motionless, poised end of winter, before the real shift to spring.

object in path

tight fence

hole ahead

Hardly poetry in motion out there — forgot to illustrate the dumbest-looking move: toe of boot contacts tip of branch which then arcs to vertical position:

snow in boots

stick trap

rolling pebble

paralysis

EAGLE BEND, DOWNSTREAM ~ A BRIGHTER DAY

INTRICATE ICE LOBES FORM ALONG FAST WATER

Light
and its effects
are always my first
aesthetic avenue. There's a
quality of light that seems "nostalgic", as though it had
arrived from some far distant past. A low-angle beam falling at the base of a tree, sometimes, or a backlit clump
of wintergrass will trigger the sensation, along with a
wash of sadness. But it's the exalted kind, not workaday
sadness — worrying, brooding, regretting — which absorbs
too much of my attention anyway, even while walking.
Much less of that now, with Sisu as a companion. Following
the direction of her attention deflects mine outwards. If I
can get beyond workaday sadness, rewards inevitably
come. I can categorize them, from the common to
the extraordinary:

1. Encountering the familiar and beloved ~ in the form of a well-known trail, prospect, tree, creature.

2. Deepening the map ~ making a new mental connection that integrates separate places into a sense of the larger place.

3. Gaining increments of knowledge ~ when I slow down enough to study or draw, I can learn the why and how of these ice lobes and stacked bubbles.

4. Entering new territory ~ the thrill of finding a new place nearby, usually from examining maps, or by setting out in a new direction from familiar ground.

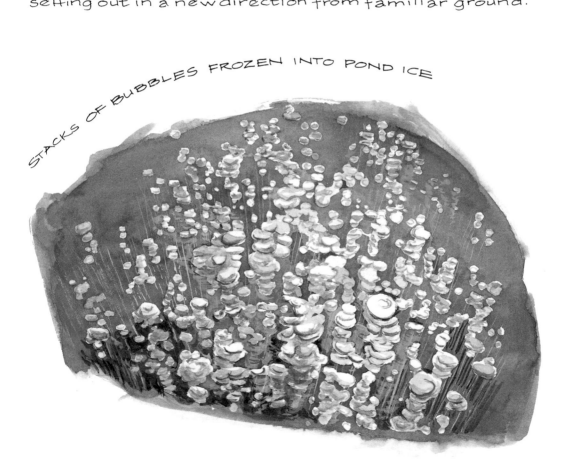

STACKS OF BUBBLES FROZEN INTO POND ICE

NOSTALGIC
LIGHT ON
OLD
COTTONWOOD
AT THE EDGE
OF THE
LONG FIELD

5. Personal ritual observances ~ as in listening for the first Swainson's thrush of the year, or watching for the thinnest crescent moon each month.

6. Out-of-time events ~ as in "nostalgic" light, but also a more mysterious displacement (see Chapter Three).

7. Sudden illuminations ~ moments of glimpsing an underlying pattern, order and unity; a sense of wholeness or completion.

8. Amazing events ~ being lucky enough to see a badger undulating across the prairie, or finding the fresh prints of a mountain lion.

9. Real discoveries — these are only personal discoveries, but they carry the same thrill that a pioneering scientist must know. One involved watching a hornet remove the cambium layer of a river birch branch to make paper pulp for its nest. I'd wondered about the distinctive oblong divots on similar branches for years but never knew what made them.

Workaday sadness is diluted and absorbed outdoors in the "more than human" world. Spirits are revived by the constancy of the real. And what do we really know of all this — the substance of light, the inner lives of creatures, the forming and dissolving of clouds and mountains, the countless events playing out simultaneously, ceaselessly? I find it soothing to be rendered insignificant. And am cheered just to be at home on the planet, upright and walking around, in the midst of the vast unknowable.

SISU IN THE PURITY OF HER ANIMAL NATURE

OLD
SNOW

holes around
bases of stems
where they've
conducted
heat....

imprints
where
blades of
grass have
sprung up
from
confinement

NEW
SNOW

humps
and pillows
Wee mounds
cover the
tips of
grass blades

Snow
heaps up
along stems
of mustard.

What do I trust?

• The purity of animal nature • The ineffable but reassuring steadiness of the present • Light and its phenomena • The solidity of the planet • The reliability of the seasons, of gravity, of three dimensions • The ingenuity of evolution • The creatureliness of humans • The will to persist in all living things • The basic integrity of the mind/senses • Certain music and other forms of artistic vision

1. salsify
2. alfalfa seeds
3. ? a mustard
4. wild sunflower
5. yarrow
6. ? a dock

3.

4.

2.

1.

need some

5.

6.

roughage.

Last night, after the Chinook wind arrived, Sisu and I went out for a last walk, joined by neighbor Shorty's dog. Both of them grew alarmed as we approached the picnic area, soon locating a set of tracks and examining them with grave concentration. I was able to isolate several clear prints. They had to be recent, since the temperature had risen and softened the snow only in the last half-hour. These were detailed, crisp impressions. As the light diminished, the dogs grew more anxious, bristling and looking over their shoulders.

used claws to climb slippery incline

Next morning we followed the trail as it wove through dense brush, beside half-fallen trees that would make ideal ambush perches. Surely this was a mountain lion, considering the tracks and the dogs' reactions.

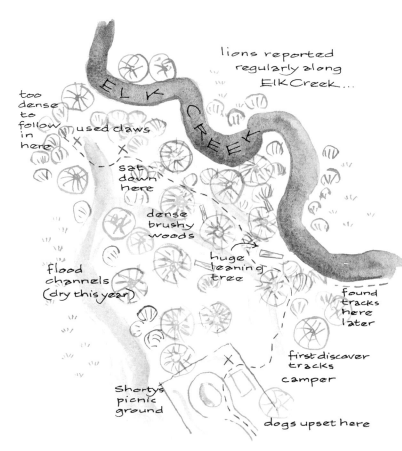

lions reported regularly along Elk Creek...

ELK CREEK

too dense to follow in here

used claws

sat down here

dense brushy woods

flood channels (dry this year)

huge leaning tree

found tracks here later

first discover tracks

camper

Shorty's picnic ground

dogs upset here

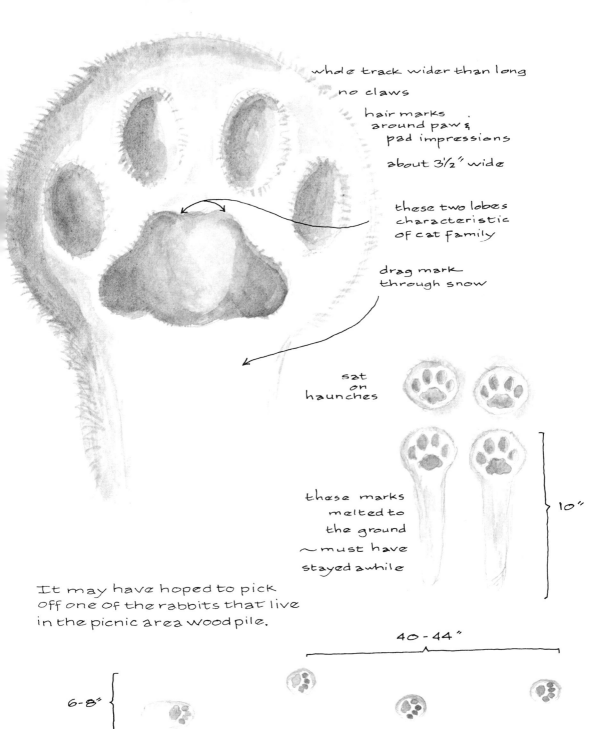

whole track wider than long

no claws

hair marks
around paw &
pad impressions

about 3½" wide

these two lobes
characteristic
of cat family

drag mark
through snow

sat
on
haunches

these marks
melted to
the ground
~ must have
stayed awhile

10"

It may have hoped to pick
off one of the rabbits that live
in the picnic area wood pile.

40 - 44"

6-8"

Puddles in the corral, snow all melted by the
Chinook. Horses doze, shifting from hip to hip.
Magpie arrives, one who often makes an
afternoon tour of the corral. Gleans a few
bits of grain, then flies far across the fields
to a distant fencepost.

I know all this — it's the familiar beloved.

CHAPTER THREE

Willow Creek

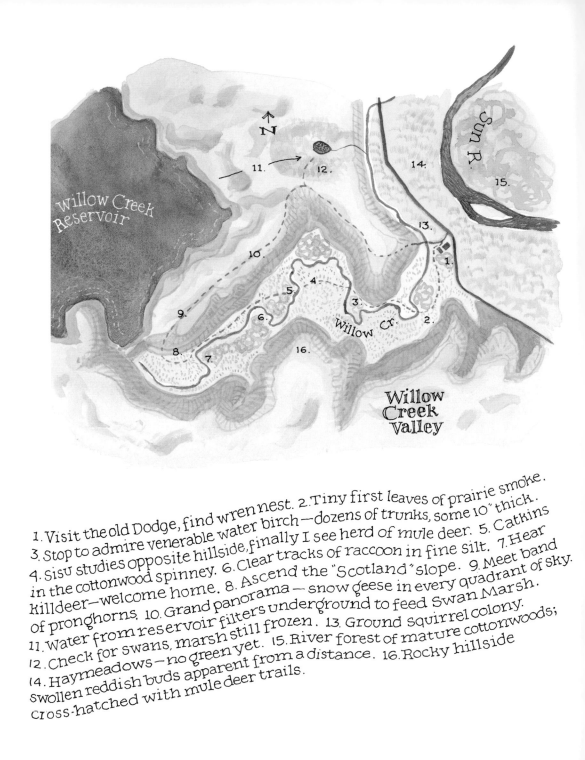

1. Visit the old Dodge, find wren nest. 2. Tiny first leaves of prairie smoke. 3. Stop to admire venerable water birch—dozens of trunks, some 10" thick. 4. Sisu studies opposite hillside, finally I see herd of mule deer. 5. Catkins in the cottonwood spinney. 6. Clear tracks of raccoon in fine silt. 7. Hear killdeer—welcome home. 8. Ascend the "Scotland" slope. 9. Meet band of pronghorns. 10. Grand panorama — snow geese in every quadrant of sky. 11. Water from reservoir filters underground to feed Swan Marsh. 12. Check for swans, marsh still frozen. 13. Ground squirrel colony. 14. Haymeadows—no green yet. 15. River forest of mature cottonwoods; swollen reddish buds apparent from a distance. 16. Rocky hillside cross-hatched with mule deer trails.

t's easy to avoid human debris in this country, and I usually do. The oldest homesteads retain their dignity, but caved-in barns, rusting Mustangs and abandoned tableware strike too close to home. All attest to the "bust" end of the boom-and-bust cycle that has dogged Montana's settled history. Artifacts can be depressing if you feel perilously situated yourself. The relics here on Willow Creek don't project futility because the owners of this ranch seem to revere them — they've carefully arranged vintage mowers by the ranch gate. One old hand pointed out that the tongue of this mower was rebuilt to fit a tractor instead of a team. Oxidizing to a state beyond rust, its blue patina complements a March day.

This old barn sports a new silver roof. Nearby, deeply settled, is a handsome Dodge truck from the 40s — a truck of many vivid and cheering colors (at least to me, in my end-of-winter color starvation). Home-done welds show where it was repaired and converted to suit its owner. Enterprising animals have further converted it: I find a golf-ball-size hornets' nest in the cab, seed caches on the floorboards, and
a house wren's nest tucked into a broken headlamp.

I've yet to meet the owners of the ranch, who live in Butte. They haven't owned it for long, but their attention to the buildings and the relics suggests that they will care for the land as well. Badly overgrazed in the past, the streambanks are stripped, trampled and eroded. Invasive species that cows don't eat, like wild rose and snowberry, have moved in to replace the over-taxed grasses. The place needs to rest. If I owned it, I'd fence cattle out of the stream and move them from pasture to pasture more often, to mimic the migratory pattern of bison, with whom these grasslands evolved. But then, I wouldn't run cattle at all. I'd be content with a couple of horses and an abundance of wild creatures. Maybe some chickens.

Crossing and recrossing the meanders of the creek on the old ice, I find I'm slowing down, stopping often to listen. This is the beginning of The Welcome, where day by day, in the increasing light, I expect to hear the notes of birds

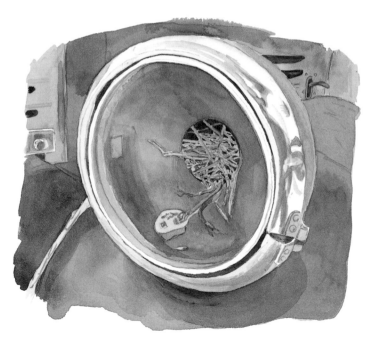

newly returned to their nesting grounds. Each year for decades I've kept a dated list of the progress of spring, including weather, plants and animals. Later in the year it reverts to running commentary, but from now until July, a list is the only way to keep up with the density of events.

Here's an anticipated note: the plaintive minor of a killdeer. In the stony confusion of the streambed, a fragment seems to shift. Now I see the black and white banding of the throat, so like the antelope up on the prairie plateau. A pair of killdeer who have settled for the night, weary from the flight in.

Their cryptic patterns work well to conceal them against this background.

BOULDER IN QUIET WATER ABOVE THE CROSSING:
INTERLOCKING ZONES OF TRANSPARENCY & REFLECTION.

THE WELCOME ~ February~April

Feb. 20 – male ground squirrels in evidence.

Feb. 25 – a robin alone, looking doubtful.

Feb. 27 – starlings begin their confusing mimicry, raising hopes of birds who aren't back yet. Raven: "tok-tok-tok."

Mar. 1 – single redwing blackbird. Half-hearted Cassin's finch song.

Mar. 3 – Canada geese restless, sometimes paired off.

Mar. 5 – horned larks singing on prairie.

Mar. 7 – warm day, flying insects including bees.

Mar. 15 – battle chases among male ground squirrels. Ravens wait for road kill.

Prairie smoke ~ new leaves, green; last year's leaves, brown; still older leaf, gray

Mar. 18 - juncos filtering through, no trilling yet.
Mar. 19 - first few trumpeter swans. Robins begin nest-site search.
Mar. 20 - golden eagle courtship flights.
Mar. 21 - Killdeers are back. Catkins opening, strong "buckwheat pancakes & maple syrup" smell from cottonwood buds.
Mar. 22 - Snow geese increase. Redtails are back.
Mar. 25 - sandhill cranes in/on snow, Redwing Slough.
Mar. 26 - 53 trumpeter swans at Redwing Slough. First bluebirds are back.
Mar. 29 - enormous flights of snow geese - thousands

Catkins emerging from sticky buds

in a single flock. Meadowlarks singing regularly.
Apr. 5 - a kestrel. Flickers sing dawn to dusk. Easter daisies.
Apr. 8 - tree swallows, pasqueflowers. Curlews return.
Apr. 10 - full complement of ducks. Geese nesting.
Apr. 13 - snowstorm. Bluebirds en masse.
Apr. 15 - great blue herons. Explosion of spring.
Apr. 18 - snipes winnowing. Visible green-up.
Apr. 20 - new bird for me: McCown's longspur, on prairie. Floats down from sky like angel in B movie, singing.
Apr. 25 - full bird din now with geese, curlews, cranes, snipes, meadowlarks, swans and the ceaseless whickering of flickers. (These are just the loud ones.)

Pausing above the deep pool with its eloquent single boulder, I find that I've been "transported" to Scotland. It's an uncanny sensation, a bit frightening; one that I've experienced only a handful of times in my life. The identity of the place has changed. I'm walking in another, yet strangely familar landscape, whose Gaelic name I'm about to pronounce. I've never been to Scotland, but have no doubt that's where I am now. It's a relocation at once convincing, seamless and eerie.

I've turned away from the creek, to drift up a long Scottish slope, where the light on the boulders is lyrical and moving. Then a band of pronghorns appears and breaks the spell; only a sort of post-dream wistfulness remains.

Sisu, with her customary diplomacy, avoids eye-contact with this group, though one steps out of the herd toward us and makes a sound like a snapped banjo string. Ever curious, they'll watch us pass without panic — unless we have accidentally divided the band. We haven't; their body language expresses security.

We leave them and climb, stream-course falling away below and mountains rising in the west.

SOMETIMES WE FIND SHED SHEATHS FROM A PRONGHORN'S "HORNS" — A SORT OF FUSED HAIR.

Re-emergence of the ground squirrels heralds a feverish time for Sisu, who explodes out of the truck in pursuit. Never far from a burrow entrance, they dive and chirp warnings from within, maddening to her. She plunges her muzzle into the hole, inhaling huge draughts of rodent essence, then voices her frenzy and desperation in strangled barks.

These are Richardson's ground squirrels, the dimmer-witted of the two species on the Front — the one that most often gets decimated on the roads, used for target practice, rapt by raptors and picked off by coyotes. Sisu hasn't learned to catch them unless they're hampered by snow. The poor creatures seem to have

no advantages beyond burrows and large families. They don't even run very fast, and have evolved a peculiar adaptation to life on the prairies, which is to half-leap every few paces, lifting head and shoulders to see above the grass—not at all effective in crossing highways. Everyone around here calls them gophers, though they aren't. And they seem to be confused with prairie dogs, now considered endangered. In Wyoming we called them "picket pins" because, upright, they resemble the stakes used to tether horses for grazing.

Only the male squirrels are above ground yet, engaging in bloody dominance battles.

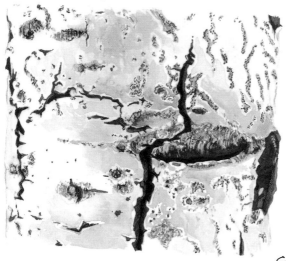

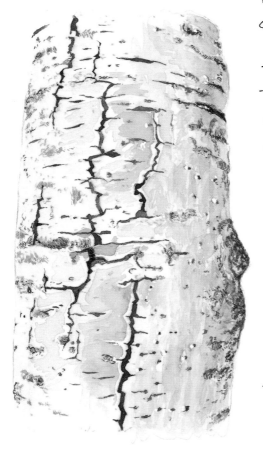

WE WESTERNERS REVERE THE COTTONWOOD; IT'S OUR ONLY GRAND DECIDUOUS TREE. WE OVERLOOK ITS TENDENCY TO WIND-PRUNE BUSHELS OF TWIGS, TO DIE BY INCHES OVER DECADES, TO BREAK IN HALF IN A GALE. AFTER A TREE LOSES ITS TOP, A SIDE BRANCH WILL BEGIN TO GROW VERTICALLY AND TAKE OVER AS THE CROWN ~ AN AWKWARD LOOK. WE HAVE THREE SPECIES AROUND HERE, THE BLACK, THE PLAINS AND THE NARROWLEAF COTTONWOODS, CONTENT WITH THE SAME RIVER BOTTOM AND STREAMSIDE HABITATS.

YOUNG COTTONWOODS HAVE SMOOTH BARK, USUALLY GRAY, BUT SOMETIMES WITH THIS RICH BUTTERED-TOAST COLOR. IF THE BEAVERS DON'T REAP THEM, OTHER VAGARIES

BEGIN TO APPEAR – NICKS, FISSURES, POCKS AND RASHES. THESE VIOLATIONS OF THE BARK HEAL, MOSTLY, WITH A SILVERY SCAR TISSUE THAT'S MUCH MORE LIKE BARK AS WE KNOW IT. EVENTUALLY THE TRUNK BECOMES ALL OVER CORRUGATIONS WHILE THE UPPER LIMBS AND TWIGS REMAIN SMOOTH. WINTER-PRUNED LIVE TWIGS ARE A FAVORITE TREAT FOR THE HORSES. ON THE HOMEWARD CURVE OF A WALK, I GATHER ARMLOADS OF THEM, FLING THEM INTO THE CORRAL AND WATCH THE TWO GELDINGS STRIP THE BARK AND EAT THE BUDS. LATER, THEY PLAY GAMES WITH THE SMOOTH WHITE STICKS.

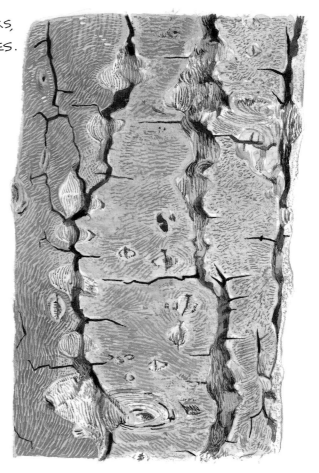

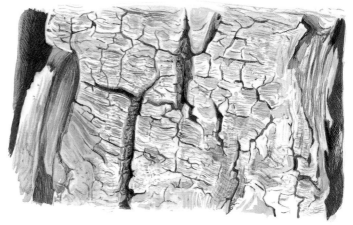

A band of mule deer grazes
on the bouldery canyon
wall above us. Last year's
fawns are stouter; they've
lost the delicacy they had in
the fall. They're in their
graceless phase, to the
degree that any deer can
be graceless. They attempt
to jump barbed-wire fences
now, like their elders,
instead of wriggling
under the strands.
I quail to
see it.

CHAPTER FOUR
Redwing Slough

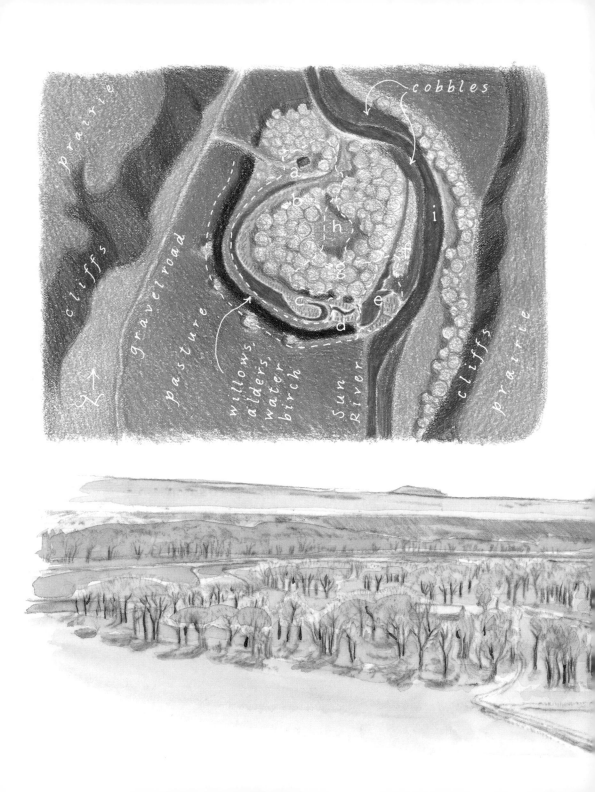

For a year I called this place simply "The Swamp" (which makes it sound far more remote and impenetrable than it is), then I read David M. Carroll's book *Swampwalker's Journal*, and learned how many distinct kinds of wetlands there are. Technically this is a freshwater marsh, but the flooded part of it occupies an old meander of the Sun River — a slough — and brims with red-winged and yellow-headed blackbirds in season. The flooded slough is impounded by terraced beaver dams, but springs must feed it, since the water level seems unaffected by drought. It's reliably green and lush all summer, teems with creatures, and is a heart-poundingly exciting place to be right now, at the height of The Welcome.

REDWING SLOUGH

a. barn (unused)
b. bald eagle nest
c. cattail zone
d. major beaver dam

e. lower ponds (low dam)
f. young cottonwoods
g. red tailed hawk nest
h. central meadow
i. deepest water

SIDE BRANCH BECOMES MAIN TRUNK

1. open water slough
2. marshy margins (sedges, rushes)
3. wire rush beds
4. cattails
5. wetland shrub zone (alder, willow, birch)
6. dam outflow channel (aquatic plants)
7. meadows (native grasses)
8. meadows (planted hay mix)
9. spring-fed ponds
10. mature cottonwoods
11. young cottonwoods (since '64 flood)
12. cobble bar
13. barn (nature/human collaboration)
14. cutbanks (along the river)
15. river itself

Though I love having it to myself, Redwing Slough cries out to be a nature center or an outdoor lab. Its curves give it a "diorama" feel, and it encompasses a textbook's worth of habitat zones, all within 100 acres:

Any school kid could be intrigued by such variety. Plus there's a dump full of antique bottles and old-style barbed wire, a bleached bull carcass and an active bald eagle nest.

SISU WADES IN GENTLY, TENTATIVELY. THE DUCKS ARE
UNRUFFLED, IN FACT THEY BEGIN TO SWIM TOWARD
HER, AT WHICH POINT SHE WADES BACK OUT.

One bank of the slough is a grassy sward, easy to navigate even for a bumbler. The principal beaver dam is old enough to be reedgrass-grown and wide enough to stroll across. From a perch in the middle of the dam, you have a privileged view of hundreds of nesting blackbirds, elusive ducks like cinnamon teal and shovelers, working muskrats, basking turtles, hunting herons and nest-sitting sandhill cranes. Audible but rarely visible (unless they fly) are snipe, wee sora rails and the deeply mysterious bittern. At this season, there's never a duckless, hawkless or gull-less interval in the sky. Sound extends my habitat range ∼ I can hear curlews and meadowlarks on the distant prairie uplands.

As Sisu harasses (or is harassed by) the ground squirrels in the meadows I have a rare chance to be first at the verge of the slough. Three trumpeter swans dwarf the channel. Low-angle sun emphasizes the solidity

of their backs, a dense unfeatherlike shield, almost waxy. They drift in a nimbus of white light. Gestures of their necks, so apparently gracious and courtly; a bow, an inclination of the head, so polished and restrained.

A swan thrashes along the surface of the slough, broad feet slapping, churning spray. I hear wingtips percussing water, air whooshing through pinions... and a clicking sound—what is it? The big quills of the flight feathers rattling together.

It's this last sound that makes me understand viscerally how massive these birds are. They gain altitude slowly, curving over the cottonwood forest, then above clifftop level. I see them immaculate against an approaching squall.

Alongside the cattail marsh, the din of blackbirds is over-powering. The ear can concentrate on the first liquid notes of the redwings and hear an unbroken sheet of that sound. Or it can isolate the tortured "bra-a-a-a-ck's of the yellow-heads, and become immersed in that braying raspberry.

Here, now, though, something strange is happening. The noise abruptly subsides into a uniform, bubbling hiss, a sound I've never heard before. I'm not the cause of their alarm, nor is Sisu. The most we've ever elicited is an angry "pee-ur" or "clack" if we stray too near a nest. Then I see—there's a prairie falcon overhead. The bizarre seething continues until the falcon is well out of sight, then cacophany resumes.

PRAIRIE FALCON OVERHEAD

It stands to reason that birds whose congregated voices are so loud would choose as their unified alarm note something con-trastingly quiet. Like the babble of a nightclub crowd reduced to whispers when a gang boss walks in the door. These birds must have different alarm calls for an aerial threat vs. a terrestrial one, as ground squirrels do. Yet they ignore both the local pair of red-tails and the nesting bald eagles.

I yearn to know — how would they respond to the shape of a harrier, or a sharp-shinned hawk, both of them bird-eaters? How about a snake? What would have happened if the falcon had stooped on a blackbird? Would they have escalated their common defense, or scattered in terror?

A YELLOW-HEADED BLACKBIRD, WORKING UP TO A " BRA-A-A-ACK."

" All the way north
    her neck stretches to arrive,
    and with each wing stroke her voice
    haunts a chambered throat
    with rolling horn notes we knew
    when we were wild
    and held to our mouths
    spiral horns of antelopes
    and raised them toward
    cranes across the sky.

    All the long way north,
    she paints her feathers,
    preens each night
    with beakfuls of clay
    so on her nest she will
    be earth invisible. "

                        ~ John Caddy

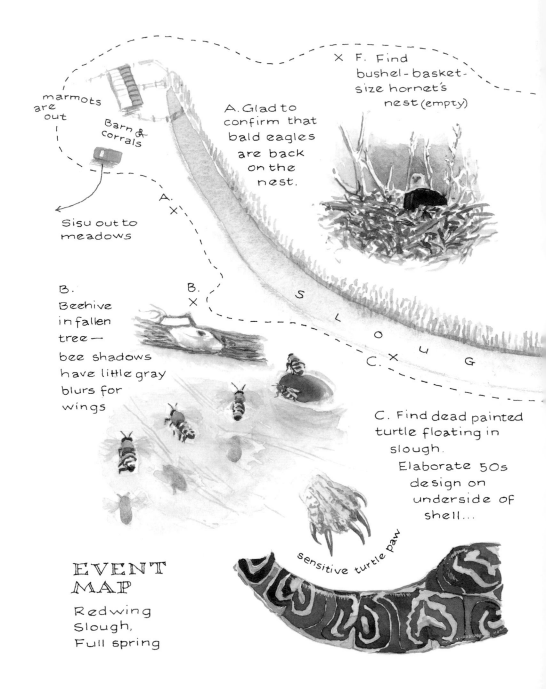

marmots are out

Barn & corrals

Sisu out to meadows

X F. Find bushel-basket-size hornet's nest (empty)

A. Glad to confirm that bald eagles are back on the nest.

A.
X

B.
Beehive in fallen tree — bee shadows have little gray blurs for wings

B.
X

S L O U G H

C.
X

C. Find dead painted turtle floating in slough.
Elaborate 50s design on underside of shell...

sensitive turtle paw

EVENT MAP
Redwing Slough,
Full spring

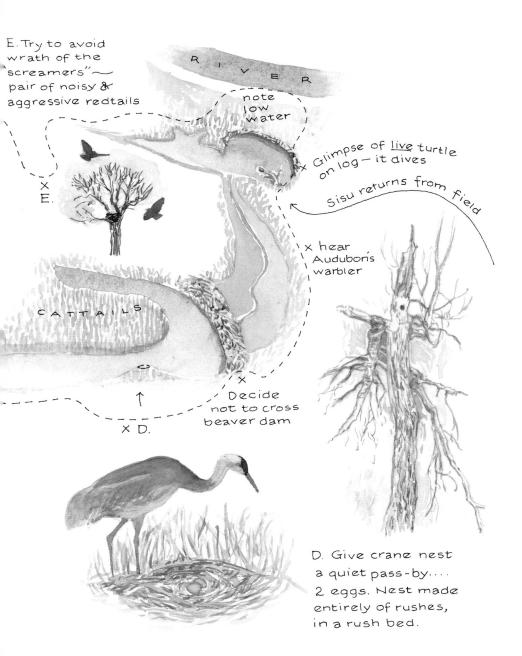

E. Try to avoid wrath of the "screamers"~ pair of noisy & aggressive redtails

R I V E R

note low water

E.

Glimpse of <u>live</u> turtle on log — it dives

Sisu returns from field

x hear Audubon's warbler

C A T T A I L S

x Decide not to cross beaver dam

x D.

D. Give crane nest a quiet pass-by.... 2 eggs. Nest made entirely of rushes, in a rush bed.

After finding the dead turtle in the slough —
limp, sodden, no longer wary and alert —
it's a joy to glimpse this quick one in the lower
ponds. It dives, I've disturbed its sun-warmed
peace. The anguish of our relation to wild
animals. To be always an object of fear —
such a sad, lonely gulf.

CHAPTER FIVE

Double Creek / Dearborn River

PASQUEFLOWER

Toward noon on our indolent mornings at Double Creek, Sisu and I slither down a shaley slope to the Dearborn River where it narrows into a series of chutes and pools. We share a lunch down here by the water where it's 10° cooler than up on the "mainland". The water level has begun to drop, exposing areas of damp sand and clammy cobbles, alive with insects. This morning I see dozens of thread-waisted wasps patroling the gravel, occasionally lighting down in their nervous glittery way. They're solitary hunting wasps, at the moment neither excavating nursery burrows (wrong surface) nor hunting caterpillars that I can see, so I'm puzzled by this assembly. Last summer, I watched one of these wasps dig a tunnel, drag a paralyzed caterpillar into it, pick up a small stone that came

avens

penstemon

geranium

from the excavation,
seal the entrance with it,
scratch sand over the spot
like a cat in a litter box, then
seize another small pebble
and use it to tamp down
the surface of the burrow.

In and around this damp
spot are also butterflies:

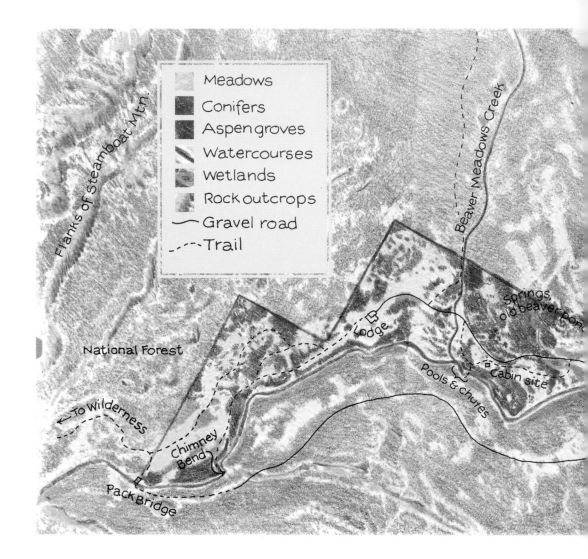

Meadows
Conifers
Aspen groves
Watercourses
Wetlands
Rock outcrops
— **Gravel road**
----- **Trail**

Flanks of Steamboat Mtn

Beaver Meadows Creek

National Forest

Lodge

Springs, old beaver pond

Pools & chutes

Cabin site

To Wilderness

Chimney Bend

Pack Bridge

checkerspots, fritillaries, blues and sulphurs, a continuous colorful rustling of them. In a sort of scrim a foot above the ground are hundreds of blue damselflies (the name "civil bluet" comes to mind) drifting about or clinging to the stems of grasses. As they shift and overlap, I see them form a series of mathematical symbols: $= + \times > <$.

Map labels:

Antler Creek
Hanging Grove
Empty Creek
waterfall
old diversion
Aspen Grove the Elder
Paintbrush Knob
Island Grove
Barn, shed, corrals
Bridge
Aspen Grove the Younger
Eastern Meadows
River
Dragonfly Pool
N
DOUBLE CREEK

Though I don't see any mating, they must have done so, because females are laying eggs in eddy that will soon become a puddle, dabbing their abdomens like fussy cake decorators. Higher up, in the air corridor above the river, dragonflies span territories, making right-angle turns.

The peripheral flash of a bird-shape turns out to be a spotted sandpiper on the far bank well above the water line, moving furtively across the ledges. Pretty soon it ducks under an arching branch of cinquefoil, and with much ruffling, squirming, rotating and panting, settles onto what must be a nest. Before long it slips away again, so I undertake to cross the river to investigate, using a driftwood limb as a staff. Sisu chooses a flat pool to swim, and is on the cliffs chasing chipmunks before I'm halfway across.

ALERT IN THE WIND

I've learned a little about wading fast water. I must ignore the urge to peer through the surface to see what my feet are doing, or I'll be mesmerized by the rushing river and lose equilibrium. Better to keep looking at the far shore, moving by feel, facing upstream, using the staff sometimes

as an anchor, sometimes
as a prop. If I get
nervous and try to
hurry, all is lost.
A douse today
would be
fine; it's hot
(though the
water is
pure snow-
melt and
heart-stoppingly
cold) — and there's a pool
just downstream from where
I've elected to cross. Still, it's
a bit scary, what with the
roaring and the weight of the
current, waist deep at one point.
My knees, already wobbly when
I gain the bank, get a second
jolt when an enormous toad
fetches up against my ankle.
It's the second toad I've
met at Double Creek
(in fact it might be the
same one). Toad wedges his
splendid fatness into a
humid rock crevice.

SLEEPING
IN
THE
WIND

Pyramid Peak

Big Meadows

view WEST into wilderness

VIEW FROM PAINTBRUSH KNOB TOWARD PYRAMID PEAK

Flanks of Steamboat Mtn. →

to Beaver meadows →

Antler Creek

from the Knob

The sandpiper nest is a rounded hollow in the dust,
with a neat rim of vegetation. It contains 4 eggs
of a color that A.C. Bent (of Bent's *Life Histories of Birds of
North America*) calls "cartridge buff", with irregular
umber scrawlings. Especially intriguing because the
bird that vacated it was a male. In spotted sand-
pipers, the females are big and aggressive, mate
with several males, lay eggs in several nests and
leave all the incubation and parenting to the guys,
while they go fishing (or bugging in this case).

That spawns fantasies
of what a swath I
could cut among the
handsome hay hands
at the Buckhorn Bar
had we sandpiper
ways: romantic
frolics in a variety
of secluded
mountain cabins
over the course of
the summer,
dropping an egg
here or there.
I'd stop in to
visit the
charmingly
precocious
hatchlings and
their devoted
fathers when I
was in the
neighborhood...

THIS LOVELY YELLOW
UMBEL UNFOLDING ~
I CAN'T IDENTIFY IT.

I pick my way along the ledges to get an elevated view of the final chute and pool. The chute is only 4 feet across but the entire river passes through it, so it must be formidably deep. As the water issues from it, all froth and tumult, it suddenly stills, at least on the surface. Underneath, it has carved out a sub-aqueous cave. Subtle whorls, visual distortions and upwelling silver bubbles show that the chute's energy is being employed deep inside this astonishing jade chamber. Trout blink on and off in the dimness, depending on how the light strikes them.

The pool is bounded by an apron of polished ledge and flows over it in a glassy arc, an excellent place to cross if you're feeling sure-footed. Reach down to part the pouring curtain, changing the uniform sound of the falls. It's on such polished surfaces that I find the mystery creature. If anyone can identify it, please let me know.

CURRENT

¼ - ½"

Earlier, in the newness of the morning we'd visited some of our favorite places on the ranch, stopping often so that I could draw plants in bloom. The time of the lewdly beautiful orchids, the shockingly cyan penstemons, sym-metries of developing flower buds, and leaves shaking out their folds is already behind us. In the past 10 days the grasses have extended their seed stalks so that the meadows are no longer a level nap, but undulant and rest-less. There are still a few blossoms on the ubiquitous Kinnikinnick, and how disarmingly beautiful they are. Heath is my favorite plant family: I admire their stocky toughness, and contrastingly fey and demure blossoms. Kinnikinnick, a wonderful name to say and write, means "mixture" in Algonquian, referring to the time when it was added to tobacco and smoked. Its Latin name, *Arctostaphylos uva-ursi*, translates (twice) as "bears' grapes", because bears eat the pretty but bland berries.

Our local lady's slipper orchid, *Cypripedium montanum*, bloomed extravagantly this year, especially in one superb creekside stand that numbered scores of stalks. Lady's slipper has a complicated life history. The tiny seeds can't germinate without the presence in the soil of a certain fungus, which both digests the seed's tough outer coat and provides the embryo with nourishing sugars. The orchid's pouch turns out to be a temporary trap for small bees, who wiggle in and buzz around until they negotiate the exit, picking up and depositing pollen in the process. The orchid apparently offers no nectar reward —hardly an inducement to try another. I always hope to hear a bee in a pouch. How mad does it get? How long is it stuck in there?

MOUNTAIN
LADY'S
SLIPPER

How do they feel when they finally break
free? A few times I've noticed neatly
chewed holes in the pouches — entry or
exit for some kind of insect. Peeved bee
on its second encounter with an orchid?
But their season has passed. Now it's
the time of squalling sapsucker infants
in hollow aspens...

CHAPTER SIX

Rodeo Day

the old sign over the ticket booth

Howdy and a Big Welcome to THE "BIGGEST LITTLE" TOWN IN THE WEST AUGUSTA, MONTANA

Our rodeo is a one-day affair, but it's been a tradition since 1935 and has a devoted following. The rodeo grounds are welcoming: picnic areas shaded by old and well-kept cottonwoods, a set of vintage bleachers, roofed and breezy. In June, the cottonwood cotton is blowing and the branches are thick with yellow warblers.

You can hear them singing in the quiet moments, when the guys are getting lined out in the chutes. Sometimes a thunder~head will rear up over the trees.

The air smells like willows and clear river water. On the grounds, there's no real boundary between contest-ants and visitors — you can walk alongside a roper limbering up, reach between the boards to pat the broncs in the holding pen (not always wise) and watch a sore-muscled bull-rider getting a massage on a portable table.

New look for cowboys: the generously cut, crispy pressed button-down oxford cloth shirt. A big improve-ment over the old torso-hugging gut-accentuating pearl-snap classic.

"May I take a closer look at your belt buckle?"
~ Bull riders aren't shy.

The Brahma bulls snooze in the pens; they're always the last event. I've seen this brindle pattern on Great Danes and bull mastiffs.

The urban cowgirl below turned heads at the rodeo today. She's a Buckle Bunny — any prospective dance partner better be sporting a big one that says "Champion" on it. On the porch at the Buckhorn after the show we have: fresh shirts, ironed jeans Budweisers, and that hungry look. Even though Augusta's "phone book" is about as big as a café menu we still manage to support three bars. The Buckhorn is where you bring the kids and let 'em mash

their fingers rolling pool balls. The Lazy B, two doors down, has an old-hotel feel and a superior dance floor. The Western's juke box is by far the best (at least to my antiquated tastes — lots of Hank Williams Sr.), and admits lots of natural light — not always an advantage in a bar.
To the right here is Spuds, the Lazy B dog. She strolls across the street to the

Western, but she never actually SLEEPS in the street, like some of the local hounds. And to the left is friend Kent, with his classic Scandinavian features and a dashing new shirt...

Gentlest gun fanatic I know...

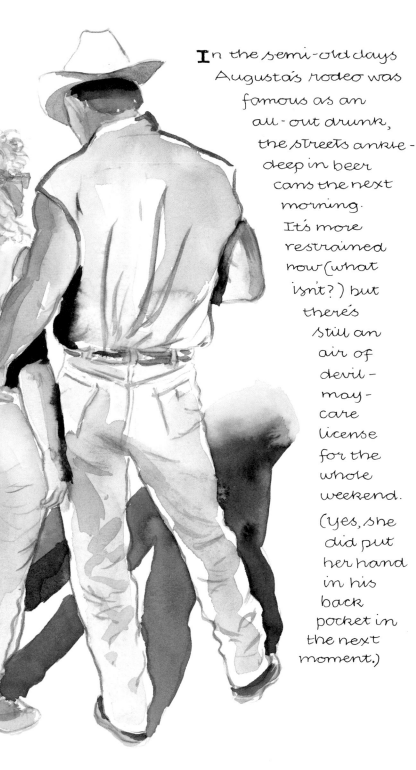

In the semi-old days Augusta's rodeo was famous as an all-out drunk, the streets ankle-deep in beer cans the next morning. It's more restrained now (what isn't?) but there's still an air of devil-may-care license for the whole weekend.

(Yes, she did put her hand in his back pocket in the next moment.)

Hannah Hinchman · From a photo of the Augusta Rodeo by Gus Wolfe

A situation in the ring that the clowns are
there to handle — but this bull moved too
fast. The cowboy, much hampered by his
elaborate chaps, made it to the fence just
in time . . . . .

CHAPTER SEVEN

Sun River Game Range

This is the cowless Eden of the Sun River Game Range (officially known as the "Sun River Wildlife Management Unit").

Flowers, insects, spiders~ grasshoppers bold and concealed, still wingless, easy to stalk. Big thistles packed with beetles. Virescent green metallic bees loaded with pollen, apple green crab spiders with rose-colored patches. Thirteen miles closer to the mountain front, 800 feet higher than Augusta, I'm surprised to find that I've risen into a sultry air layer, the kind that coaxes buds to open and goads insects into frenzied activity.

I'm not phobic about cows, since their profitable presence is what has kept the Front as open as it is. Still, a chance to walk in a place that cows never touch shows me how severe their effects can be, especially in a dry year. Here, the bunch grasses are luxuriant, and flowers of many species bloom in dense swathes. It seems miraculous that 20,000 acres of superb grassland has been allowed to go uneaten.

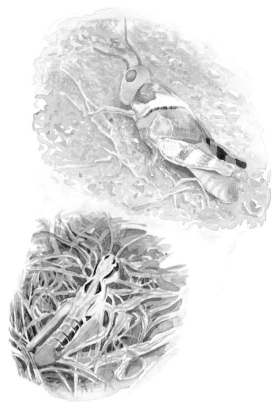

Even more miraculous is that it's open to the public, but nobody's here. On all but the rarest days, Sisu and I see only the Manager, sole employee of the Game Range, a quiet guy with a big friendly dog (Bubba). Sometimes he'll warn me if a grizzly is frequenting a certain drainage. There are no obvious attractions beyond soul-slaying views: no stellar trout streams, no fishable lakes. In an area that could contain 23 Central Parks there are just 4 domesticated creatures. Unlike Wyoming, where I came of age, Montana's public land

is mostly confined to mountain fastnesses. It's no wonder that ambitious ranchers claimed all the productive grass-land along the Front. The Game Range is not "leftover" land, like so much that became part of the Forest Service and the Bureau of Land Management. It had to be bought back and restored to the Commons. And it was local people, not government agencies, who led the way.

The Front was the high plains' most coveted bison range long before the whites arrived. Chinook winds keep the snow from accumulating on the prairies, and sheltering river valleys fan out from the mountains. The Front supported astonishing concentrations of game animals, not just bison, but also elk and bighorn sheep. And of course their predators, like the famed plains grizzly that so plagued Lewis and Clark.

By 1900, with nothing to check the hunters, the bison had vanished, elk persisted only in remnant groups high in the mountains, deer and bighorn sheep were almost gone. In the next quarter-century, under the protection of the first game regulations, the herds began to rebound.

In the winter of 1926-27 elk appeared on the foothills of the Front again after a long absence. But their winter range had all been claimed for cattle. Instead of simply shooting them (which would have been legal) the ranchers attempted to herd them back into the high country. With the help of local landowner and Forest Ranger Bruce Neal, cooperative elk-herding went on for 17 years. But the elk overgrazed the few high ridges left to them, competing with bighorn sheep whose numbers plummeted. And the elk wouldn't stay in the snowy backcountry, much like the bison

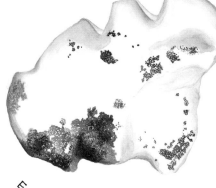

ARTIFACT FOUND IN THE CENTRAL MEADOW

EXPOSED SURFACE

UNDERSIDE

NOTCHES STAND OUT AS "CRAFTED." USED POSSIBLY TO SOFTEN LEATHER OR RAW-HIDE THONGS? OR TO SMOOTH ARROW SHAFTS? THE STONE IS DEEPLY EMBEDDED IN THE SOIL.

who migrate out of Yellowstone Park these days.
In 1948, two big ranches came on the market. They lay
directly astride major migration trails to the plains.
They were, in fact, the very ground that the elk had been
trying to reach for 17 years. With the threat of out-of-
state buyers, Bruce Neal convinced a couple of local
philanthropists to make the down payment, until the
ranches could be secured by the Game and Fish depart-
ment. Over the years, more private, federal and state
land accrued to the Game Range. Now it's a tremendous
sweep of country that stretches from the forested hem
of the Sawtooth, east through the sandstone and lava
ridge country and out
onto the open
prairie.

A
pioneering
collaboration
it seems
to me.
One
that
shows
the locals
to be more
enlightened
than they'll
normally
admit to.

LOCO WEED IN THE ROCKS

The book of Augusta history where I learned about the Game Range goes on to say that Bruce Neal's successor wanted to "help people enjoy and understand the many values of the Range." At one time organized school groups came on winter expeditions to see the elk. According to my neighbor, the local game warden, "organized school groups" devolved into an SUV free-for-all, hounding the winter-stressed elk. Now the place is completely closed to human visitors from December 1st to mid-May, when for a few days horn-hunters swarm it together shed antlers (sold as aphrodisiacs to Asian buyers).

No elk hereabouts in summer; they're way back in the Bob Marshall wilderness. But their scat is everywhere, practically a pavement of pellets. Watching the ground, teaching myself to pick out cryptic grasshoppers, I meet a favorite creature ~ a jumping spider. I call this one the gray-flannel-business-suit spider, common ground dweller out here in the foothills. A member of the genus Poultontella? Jumping spiders are cat-like in their stalks and pounces. They can see at a distance too, and this one appears to be looking up at me, holding its first pair of legs in a defensive attitude.

...GENERAL IMPRESSION OF
A FOREST OF ANTLERS
AGAINST THE SKY....

Keen eyesight complicates courtship, if your potential mate is a predator and a cannibal. Males dance before females, waving pedipalps and first legs in disco gestures, signalling, hypnotizing, mollifying.

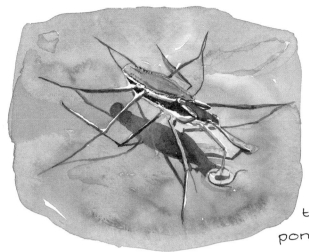

We descend into Barr Creek Valley. Its basic shape is glacial, probably excavated by a high-volume ice melt stream. Now the valley is half-filled up with soil, tiny Barr Creek meandering through it. There's a beaver pond every hundred yards or so. I realize, suddenly, that it must have been the beavers who built up all this soil. Thousands of years of beaver dams impounding silt.

Perfect light to watch water striders and their deft use of surface tension. They're amorous today. Are those courtship ripples being generated by the male? Surprised to see that the mated pair dimples the surface less than a lone strider. Weight distributed over 8 legs? The male is a puny thing — worn to a nub, I would say.

A male kingfisher comes to perch on a silvery stub near me, his reflection darker than he. He's far from his usual lowland riverbottoms, but seems perfectly matched to this streamlet and its rush-margined pools.

On a ridge with a view toward the Sawtooth, I'm in the territory of the limber pine. Many, even most are dead or dying from a combination of drought and blister rust, a disease that has decimated the whitebark pines (favorite grizzly food) in Glacier Park. Since the bears don't venture onto the plains as much as they did in earlier times, the death of the limber pines probably won't affect them. But what will become
of all these

yellow-pine chipmunks? (Sisu has treed six of them since we started walking.) And what about the Clark's nutcrackers, who have such an intimate relationship with the limber pine? A naturalist tells me that limber pines are denser now than they have been in recorded memory, the result of fire suppression. Blister rust doesn't concern him; he expects it to cull the species to its "proper" density — whatever that is. Scientists don't focus on individuals, but I can't keep

myself from it especially if I know them.

The cone crop is stunning this year; perhaps a pheromonal response to the presence of disease, or a reaction to drought. The cones are still closed, but in a couple of months, gangs of nutcrackers will be hanging upside down, extracting the nuts. They'll stuff their throat pouches to the dimensions of pouter pigeons, then fly off to bury the nuts in caches. Some of those caches will sprout the seedlings destined to outlast the disease.

The oldest trees seem immune to it. On this ridge there are ancient specimens, magnificently whorled and wind-pruned. They are the ones that have survived centuries of fires and blights. Their few live branches are lavish with cones.

I'm proud of the old-timers who laid the groundwork for the Game Range. It was a generous gesture

toward the original ways of the country and an act of foresight. Yet any evening of the week I can find people talking with glee about the prospects for oil and gas development along the Front, though none of them have seen what it can do. Pincher Creek, Alberta, has been totally transformed. I've tried to tell these habitual xenophobes that it would fill their roads with traffic and their fishing lakes with strangers. It would

CHIPMUNK SAFE
IN LIMBER PINE'S
UPPER CAVITY...

nullify the purpose of the Game Range, if not
erase the thing itself. Even the Buckhorn wouldn't
be "theirs" anymore. Misplaced patriotism and
a head-in-the-sand attitude have dulled their
native skepticism. It baffles me that these
tough and tenacious people seem so willing to
let others determine their future.

CHAPTER EIGHT

Tank Prairie

Long-billed curlew on its nest — through binoculars I watch it flatten its neck along the ground, to avoid casting a shadow. Sisu is near the nest, but either ignores it or fails to perceive it, her mind on rodents. In this reach of grassland there must be a half dozen curlew nests, but this is the first and only I've ever found. They are the quintessential bird of summer on the prairie. Everything about them seems archaic, especially their haunting, far-carrying cries. They don't linger; by late summer they gather into big family groups, and one morning they're gone.

The beetle traverses Tumbleweed Shield Lichen, *Xanthoparmelia chlorochroa*. What I've always suspected about it turns out to be true. It doesn't grow <u>on</u> anything. No roots, no substrate. It just <u>is</u>. I bust my bifocals searching for ur-pieces of it. It's everywhere on the ground, and provides a gray-green base color to the prairie landscape.

Adjoining Tank Prairie are a couple of sections of "CRP" land (which stands for Conservation Reserve Program, though some call it "Charlie's Retirement Plan"). Ranchers are paid not to graze or cultivate these once-abused parcels. Usually they are re-seeded with wheatgrasses and nitrogen-fixing alfalfa. Hail to the hard-working alfalfa, which needs no coddling and brings forth masses of flowers even in the driest years.

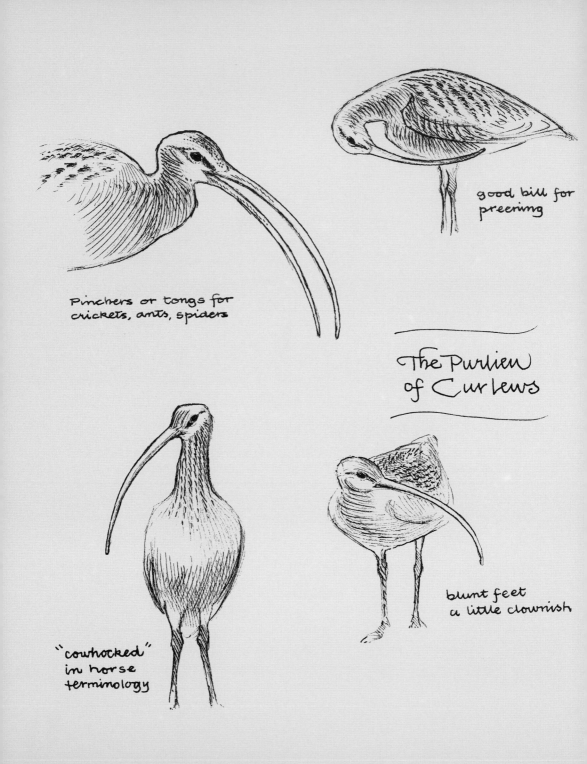

Pinchers or tongs for
crickets, ants, spiders

good bill for
preening

The Purlieu
of Curlews

"cowhocked"
in horse
terminology

blunt feet
a little clownish

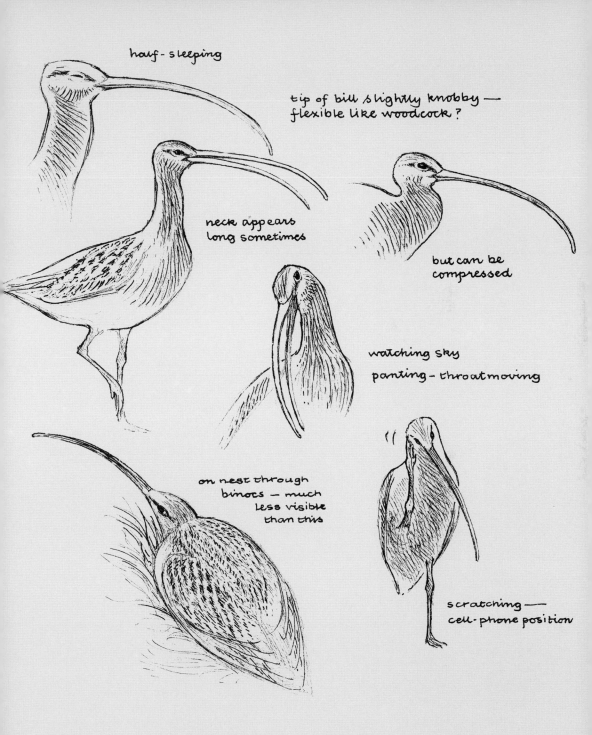

half-sleeping

tip of bill slightly knobby —
flexible like woodcock?

neck appears
long sometimes

but can be
compressed

watching sky
panting - throat moving

on nest through
binocs — much
less visible
than this

scratching —
cell-phone position

The prairie has habituated me to walking without looking down — no doubt why I trip so much everywhere else. The lure of distance, the undulating green fairway, a vague goal of visiting the cabin-size glacial boulder on a far ridge (the lower edges of which have been polished to marble smoothness by cattle, bison, maybe mammoths) — or just to set out in any direction and keep going — all this translates into a kind of beatific wanderlust.

Heightening this dawn-of-creation atmosphere are all the open-country singers and callers, especially the McCown's longspurs. Everywhere you turn, they're floating down on fixed wings, singing like Renaissance angels.

McCown's longspur

Western meadowlark

Upland sandpiper

Above, invisible, horned larks rain music, and from fenceposts meadowlarks compete with rivals half a mile away. (Our meadowlarks have a local song variation that sounds like "Weee-thihk-you're weird".)

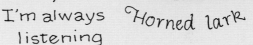

Horned lark

I'm always listening for the jubilant calliope call of the upland sandpiper, rare even in this zone of rare prairie birds. A pair sometimes joins a group of agitated curlews as they wheel and keen. But all is not beatitude on the ground. Of the many ground-squirrel burrows, only some harbor rodents. Almost every empty burrow is occupied by a big, aggressive female black widow

Black widow & egg sac

Long-billed curlew

spider,
guarding
a pearly
egg sac.
I once found
an unguarded one
of these and snipped it
open to look at the eggs.
Out poured a host of pale
spiderlings, about this size ✳
who fanned out across the
ground leaving a zone of shiny
silk anchor lines. In a minute
they'd climbed to the tops of
grasses and unfurled lengths
of flight gossamer.

grasses · tank prairie · 7.6

wiry stemlets
all heads weighted
to one side

extremely delicate

pollen dangling, ready to be blown?
...or maybe the female flowers waiting for pollen?

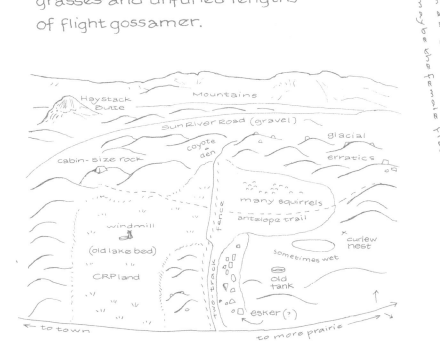

Mountains

Haystack
Butte

Sun River Road (gravel)

coyote
den

glacial

cabin-size rock

erratics

many squirrels

antelope trail

fence

windmill

x
curlew
nest

(old lake bed)

Sometimes wet

old
tank

CRP land

two-track

esker (?)

← to town

to more prairie

no plumes

this one is a bluish green

individual seed head

these seeds have plumes too (awns?)

but they're shorter and all are packed closely along a central stem

needle & thread — these seeds "screw" themselves into socks & dogs

single seed

shaft of stem splits & panicles emerge

Later this one fans out

RIDGE
OF
GLACIAL
BOULDERS
AND
OLD LAKE
FLOOR
BEYOND...

At midday, the prairie can appear almost featureless. Only low-angle light can throw into relief the hillocks, ridges and depressions — or reveal the perfectly flat surfaces on the tops of buttes, relics of ancient plains.

A midday walk can be as visually lean as a Mark Rothko canvas. No secrets given up in those hours.

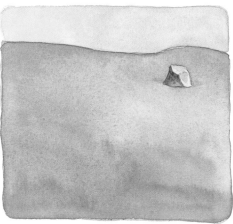

↑ This is the only chance I ever get to be long-legged. Feel like a haloed Colossus striding east.

The flat-light midday prairie landscape as a paragon of Zen design: sky, ground, the line where they meet, and a single rock.

HAYSTACK BUTTE & LAST PRAIRIE LIGHT

" THE LAST OF THE GREAT OPEN PRAIRIES
ARE RAPIDLY DISAPPEARING; AND WITH
THEM ARE GOING THE CURLEWS, THE
MARBLED GODWITS, THE UPLAND PLOVERS,
THE LONGSPURS AND A HOST OF OTHER
BIRDS THAT CAN NOT STAND THE
ENCROACHMENTS OF AGRICULTURE."

ARTHUR CLEVELAND BENT ~ 1929

SCARY LITTLE AUTOMATONS

As soon as the grasses produce their seed stalks, the prairie begins to turn gold. Now the long-awned panicles of needle & thread grass are flex-ible and feathery. But when the seeds ripen and detach, those awns bend, spiral and screw themselves into whatever they snag on. I left a tangled handful of them on the truck seat one

NEEDLE & THREAD SEEDS...

day; next morning they were all needle-end-down, sewing themselves into the upholstery.

Deep into a long walking meditation on the prairie, on and on, sun nearly down, storm breaking up in the north, fir-needle coolness ponding in the low spots, polleny warmth radiating from the knoll summits. To the next ridge, then. Sisu wants to go. Shadowy form of familiar short-eared owl on a fencepost, launches again into buoyant flight.

Ear Mountain blue on the northern horizon.
See the first bat of the night. Hear the jingle
of Sisu's collar tags as she returns in the gathering
dark....

CHAPTER NINE

The Farewell

In late August, pickups coming out of the mountains are usually full of wood. At home, it will be cut to length, split and stacked. Chainsaws drone from August till hunting season starts near the end of October.

Fall to winter is an ebbing, a diminishment. Creatures vanish quietly, like guests slipping out of a party. Grasshoppers sit on the doorstep in the morning frost, where they were the night before when cold immobilized them, and hop again at midday.

The sun runs south with frightening speed in the fall. At this latitude (close to Canada) the light change feels extreme to me: the day is disorientingly long in summer, and dawn comes in the middle of the night. From November to February, the light is crepuscular even at noon. But at least the sun is out. This is a largely sunny place.

Some years the waterfowl migration is concentrated and thrilling: 10,000 snow geese overhead at once.

EARLY FALL, AND THE BARLEY FIELD WEST OF MY HOUSE HAS BEEN CUT AND ROLLED INTO 1-TON BALES. THE MOUNTAIN FRONT STILL HAS ITS DEEP-TONED SUMMER ASPECT.

And you can be sure of the late fall vision of trumpeter swans barely visible in a snowy sky.

THE STORM BEGINS AS A SERIES OF SQUALLS AT SUNSET BUT ENGULFS THE FRONT BY NIGHTFALL.

We get enough early snows to prepare us. Usually the mountains are doused head to toe at least once in September, so we see miles and miles of dun prairie juxtaposed against

NEXT MORNING THE MOUNTAINS LOOK WEIGHTLESS,
KIN TO SKY RATHER THAN EARTH.

celestially blue and white peaks. The early snows
melt off, then our relatively austere version of fall
color begins. Stream course cottonwoods turn a
restrained bronze, sometimes freezing to brown before
they reach their peak. We have our passages of yellow
aspen, but nothing like the southern Rockies. Lowly shrubs
do most of the color work in the fall. Chokecherries,

Cornus, wild rose, willows, currants; these distinguish themselves in turn.

The birds still here after the leaves have fallen are going to stay: wind-driven flocks of horned larks on the prairie, solitary flickers, snipe, kingfishers in the sheltered areas. And the ever-companionable magpie on the fencepost.

Sisu's undercoat has grown in thick and soft. I fill the drawers with turtlenecks and fleece, and bring out the wooden bowl that holds gloves for every task and hats for every condition.

RIPE CHOKECHERRIES HAVE BEEN EATEN LONG
BEFORE THE LEAVES BLAZE FORTH.

One stiff wind denudes the cottonwoods and I
remember how much I love their skeletal shapes,
all the grotesqueries there to puzzle over again.
The landscape leaches toward a neutral palette,
so that the odd blaze of a weed stem can seem
like the needle's eye of all color. It's the time of
the year for burrs, too: an unknown, sharp-spined,
viciously entangling one that mats the horses'
tails and forelocks, and the more benign wild
licorice, visible and avoidable in its bright red-brown.
At home, Sisu works tirelessly to remove them.
The area around her bed is a minefield for wool socks.

CHOKECHERRIES BEFORE THE BIRDS GET THEM ...

Hunting season is
the apotheosis of
the year for the
locals, the time
when they live
out their myths
about themselves
(ranching is not
myth to them).

B U R R S . . .

THE BAD ONE

THE NOT-SO-BAD ONE

GOLDENROD GALL. THE PLANT CREATES THIS CHAM-
BER TO ISOLATE THE LARVA OF A TINY WASP.

MUSKRATS WORK LONG HOURS AT THIS SEASON, HAR-
VESTING WINTER FOOD AND LODGE MATERIAL. SISU
CAN HEAR THE SUBTLEST OF GNAWINGS AND RUSTLINGS
FROM THE CATTAILS AND RUSH BEDS. FROM THE BIG
BEAVER DAM AT REDWING SLOUGH SHE WADES INTO
DEEP MUCK, BUT KNOWS IT'S POINTLESS TO SWIM
AFTER THEM. SHE STUDIES THE WATER SURFACE,
SINCE MOVING REFLECTIONS ARE OFTEN ADVANCE
WARNING OF A TRAVELING MUSKRAT.

Hunting season is by far the most festive, active time of the year for both men and women. (Maybe women rejoice at how it breathes vigor into their men... I'd rather not think about it.) There are always out-of-town guests, and people take off into the wilderness for a week or more. Main Street is lined with horse trailers, the Buckhorn lot is full every night, the Game Check Station becomes a social hub of the town.

Privately I cheer for the familiar groups of mule deer and whitetails who find refuge on private land that is closed to hunting. Most ranchers

THE GAME RANGE AFTER HUNTING SEASON. IF MY FRIEND
GUS WOLFE THE PHOTOGRAPHER HADN'T POINTED THEM OUT,
I NEVER WOULD HAVE SPOTTED THE MANY BULL ELK BEDDED
DOWN IN THE ZONE OF TREES.

post their property as off-limits with orange markers,
allowing only a few friends to hunt. Though they don't
like to admit it, they have a proprietary feel about
"their" animals.

A single rifle shot sounds like someone slamming a door in a big empty house. That is what I hope to hear. More often, the morning stillness is violated by volleys of gunshots, as though a gang of idiots were shooting randomly at a running herd. Perhaps even worse is the single shot, followed by another one four or five seconds later. Then another. And another. If these aren't the sounds of brutal ineptitude, someone please enlighten me.

GUTTED ELK ARRIVE AT THE GAME CHECK STATION, WHERE TAGS ARE INSPECTED AND INFORMATION TALLIED. IT'S EARLY MORNING, AND THERE ARE THREE OTHER TRUCKS WAITING.

orange
ear
band

wary look

muttering;
calling dog

fluorescent
vest, cut
to
accommodate
beer gut

brass
bell

Sisu and I wear fluorescent orange, of course, but it annoys us. Anyone running around with a rifle should be able to tell a deer from a person. And any Kindergartner could tell you that it's dumb to shoot at something you can't see. Orange means that there are dangerous fools at large, ready to pull the trigger when a twig snaps. Every year I hear stories of fences cut, poachers, dead cows. And I spend the months after Christmas packing out the beer cans and pizza boxes tossed from hunters' pickups. So Sisu and I make sure we aren't wandering around at dawn or dusk. We don't walk anywhere near a parked truck. We eschew the Game Range until the season closes. We stick to open country and still feel uneasy. But in two months it will be over, and the place will be ours again.

fur

fluorescent
orange
collar

We do visit Redwing Slough, when it's free of hunters' trucks. All fall the place was haunted by a gargantuan Black Angus bull. I soon discovered that he has sore hooves and is no threat, but more than once have turned to find him standing next to me in the willows.

On one of these mellow afternoons, I encountered a snipe. They usually flush, but this one didn't, perhaps mesmerized by my orange vest. I watched it sink imperceptibly from a standing position to a crouch, bright eye unblinking.

SISU
INTRIGUED
BY A MUSKRAT
PLUNGE HOLE.

DAGGER ICE
SHARDS SHOW
IT'S BEGINNING
TO RE-FREEZE.

Sisu the Finn is a snow dog, buoyant and excitable in cold weather. Her colors look right and luminous in any landscape, but against winter blue and white she's an animate bonfire.

Mice and voles move about brazenly under the snow. Sisu senses them; our walks are more than partly sub-nivean for her. She also raids the winter caches made by magpies and other birds. Once, near home, she dragged me across the corner of a field to reach a cottonwood tree, where after a brief inspection she extracted a pea-size lump of suet from a crevice of bark.

THE KIND OF ICE-EDGE SHE'S LEARNED TO AVOID...

It's great fun to visit Redwing Slough after a snow, and as the slough itself begins to freeze over. In the maze of tracks and signs, I'm always struck by how few of these animals ever travel a straight line. The mouse that zigzags, the porcupine that plows around in circles like a bison, the weasel that underlines every fallen log. Not purposeless, just thorough. And yet the overall impression when reading the

MANY MICE, OR A SINGLE BUSY ONE?

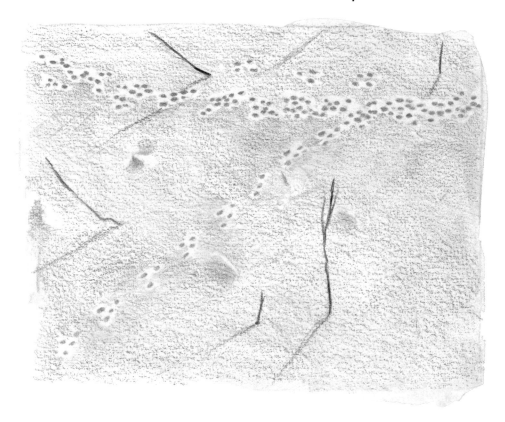

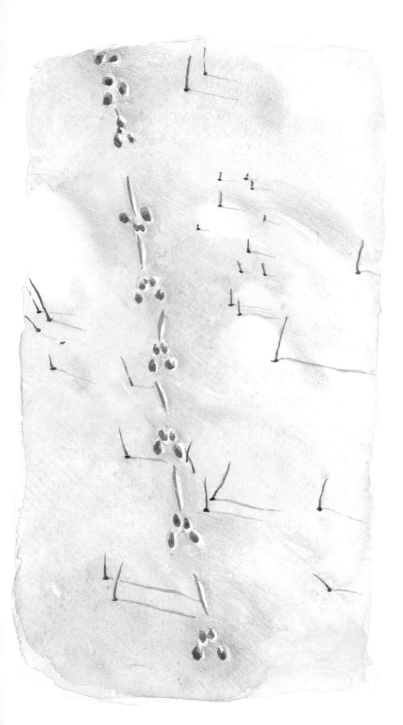

signs
is of
jigs being
danced,
crowds
bumping
into
each
other,
whole
families
visiting
door-to-
door
all
night
long.

JUST-MINTED
TRACKS IN
FLUFFY SNOW;
MUCH EFFORT
EXPENDED
IN A BOUNDING
GAIT. TAIL
PROVIDES
STABILITY,
A DRAG
NONETHELESS.

The ice on the slough goes through many permutations before the final freeze-up. There will be a layer of granular stuff, melted by afternoon. Next morning the skin will be made of dagger-like crystals (sometimes sporting great feathers of hoarfrost) broken in places by muskrats and beavers. It too will melt off.

DEER CROSSING AT THE SLOUGH, BREAKING THROUGH THE INCH-THICK ICE MUST HAVE BEEN A PAINFUL, NOISY, DESPERATE AFFAIR, JUDGING BY THE CHAOS HERE...

On a night of 10°F. or less, the ice apparently bypasses the dagger mode, and in the morning it's a clear casement, water plants and minnows visible beneath. I wait until deep winter to walk on it, because springs feed the slough and the ice is untrustworthy in all but the deepest cold.

ICE IS TREACHEROUS EVEN WHEN SOLID — NOTE THE MARKS OF SLIPPING DEER HOOVES HERE.

Sisu, however, begins testing it the moment it appears solid, and she has fallen through more than once. Now she either has learned the danger zones, or recognizes some clue of instability, because there have been none of the splash-and-yelp events I dread (since it means I'll have to go in myself and rescue she-of-the-scrabbling-claws).

HOARFROST "FEATHER" ON DAGGER ICE

We relish our
winter walks,
usually one
long ramble
when the sun
is at its zenith,
then a short foray
into the home fields
at dusk.
Daylight is brief,
we are punctual,
so these hours
have a monastic
feel, immersed in
quiet.

THE "LEONARDO COPSE"
ON THE FAR SIDE OF
THE HAY MEADOW.
IT REMINDS ME OF
DA VINCI'S DRAWING
"THE GROVE OF BIRCHES".

Back at the cabin, the horses are waiting by the barn
for their evening oats. Blue wood smoke plumes up
from the chimney, reminding me to bring in another
armload of logs. The eagles are congregating on their
night roost at Eagle Bend. A little snow drifts down
from no visible cloud. Sisu and I settle down on the
top step of the porch to watch the deer, in the last
horizontal light, enter the hay meadow.

MATERIALS & METHODS

I used gentle, forgiving Fabriano Uno Soft Press paper for almost every illustration in this book, whether watercolor, pen and ink, pastel*or colored pencil. My paints are a mix of Winsor-Newton and Daniel Smith watercolors, sometimes adding gouache by M. Graham & Co. I also relied on a few touches of Dr. Ph. Martin's Radiant Concentrated Watercolors, for hues I couldn't get otherwise.

The book is a mix of field journal sketches, pieces begun outdoors and finished in the studio, and pure studio work based on my own photos and sketch-notes. I scanned initial drawings as JPEGS so that if I wrecked the painting (as often happened) I could re-print the drawing and start over again. Sometimes I scanned a painting in its early stages, and if I didn't like how it developed, I'd re-print the early version and work right on top of it.

Finished art was scanned into my iMac, then brought into the chapter layout using Adobe PageMaker. After arranging the artwork on the page spreads, I traced around the white spaces, then scanned them and printed them out on ordinary copy paper. Then I took up the pen (Pigma Micron .005) and wrote out the text inside the shapes. The text was scanned in turn and placed on the page layouts.

*a few pastels were done on toned Ingres paper.